Too Close for Comfort

Pip Smith

DARLINGTON PRESS

Published 2013 by Darlington Press

Darlington Press is an imprint of Sydney University Press

sydney.edu.au/sup

ISBN: 9781921364440

Darlington Press
Fisher Library F03

University of Sydney
NSW 2006 AUSTRALIA
Email: sup.info@sydney.edu.au

Cover and internal images by Holiday / workbyholiday.com

Cataloguing in Publication information available from the National Library of Australia

For Tim,
who cracked open my imagination,

and Judith,
who taught me how to use it.

Contents

Contents

Foreword

Pip Smith's *Too Close for Comfort* is the inaugural winner of the Helen Anne Bell Poetry Bequest, a biennial prize for a book of poetry by an Australian female poet which deals in some way with Australian culture. This award (and future awards) has been made possible by a generous bequest from the estate of Helen Anne Bell, a former student at the University of Sydney. The inaugural award in 2013 drew a highly competitive field of entries, but the judges, joanne burns, Jill Jones and myself, felt that Pip Smith's poems were the ones which engaged most robustly and imaginatively with Australian life, concerns, and culture in the 21st century.

In *Too Close for Comfort,* Smith approaches her subjects in highly inventive ways, and this is one of the most engaging and impressive features of her work. Whether she is writing a lyric, a prose poem, a sonnet, a poem with a political message, a poem about ideas, places or people, Pip Smith is able to find original ways of presenting her material. You can sense in her work that she constantly questions and tests her language, putting it through hoops, making it roll over backwards. Smith reins in language from so many sources – songs, pop culture, the internet, to name a few – and these give the poems impressive linguistic buoyancy and make them feel absolutely contemporary. She is a most inventive phrase-maker. 'Now that's cricket' hilariously uses cricket terms and jargon as the terms of reference for a relationship: 'Do I have to spell it out? Hit. Your. Middle. Stump. / Into. My. Sticky. Wicket. What? Is my harrow drive too googly?' The poet's questioning of language and human contexts is deeply engaging, as is the fact that the poems eschew mere cleverness and don't hide behind obscurity or indulge in angst or world-weariness. Instead the poems are energetic, dynamic and extremely pleasurable while all the time engaging with serious ideas.

Pip Smith's use of form, lineation, imagery and rhythm are very finely achieved. In 'How to reason with snakes', the traditional structure of the pantoum has been reconfigured in a unique way. The various free verse arrangements of many poems have also been executed with flair and aplomb. Smith's poems are always loyal to her own voice and to the notion that poems need to be playful and inventive as they go along, open to language's transparencies as well as its self-reflexive qualities. She has an admirable ability to steer her poems away from predictable scenarios or outcomes and really give them a strong and original edge, seeking out connections and implications which make the poems stronger and which heighten their reach. *Too Close for Comfort* announces the arrival of a new and impressive voice in Australian poetry.

Judith Beveridge

Happy Christmas! (don't get tasered)

On Christmas Island there are several thousand people
locked in the raptor cage from Jurassic Park. It isn't
really the raptor cage, it's just what we call it.

What you call things is important. Language is safe
in the cool, sociopathic climes of corporate speak,
so here people aren't refugees or queue jumpers

or even asylum seekers, they're "clients". Our clients
receive a welcome pack with a free toothbrush (!)
They also get free English classes, so they can't complain,

and if they do at least it's in English. Some of our clients
are rich. They washed ashore in saris with gold bracelets
tangled in their hair, then asked for flat screen TVs (!!)

Call that needing asylum (??) Some don't say please
or thank you, and others just have heat stroke. The first boat
arrived from Holland in 1666, before Australia was called

Australia and we were all given a prison for Christmas. A man
named Goos tried to call the place "Mony Island", but it didn't
stick. In 1888 the Brits found guano under the ground, so the Crown

annexed the pile of shit and began digging it out with the help
of Malaysian slaves. Today the street signs are written in English
and Chinese, and there are shrines between weeds where footpaths

would be if the island was floating in the ACT. The locals can't grow
vegetables because bird shit + coral carcass = too much fucking lime,
so we mine it until the air is full of powdered poo and our clients

wear blackface in negative. There are many species endemic
to the island and many which aren't. There are birds with red
sacks swinging like swags from their necks. They swoop on girls

in red bikinis who have two sacks more conveniently
located on their chests. There are crazy yellow ants
and crabs the size of microwaves. It's illegal to eat them,

but the ants do anyway. I've seen whole armies crawl under
the shells. No one would ever arrest an ant, but they should.
Each November the full summer moon pulls red crabs out

of the forest and into the sea, where they breed before flooding
the shore with new arrivals. The ants eat them too. The ants eat
everything. The ants think they are above the law. The law

is abstract and hard to visualise but is perhaps a crystal orb
suspended above the ground. It is in a permanent state
of construction from the inside out, which becomes problematic

when you think about gravity. Lawyers don't have time to think
about gravity. Lawyers float through the clouds like airborne
jellyfish. Their ancient gowns pulse in the breeze. Their wigs

keep them insulated against the cold, and when they point,
electric currents shoot out the tips of their fingers. Around us
there's an electrical network of light you can't see unless

you run into it. Then you get tasered. This Christmas,
cops are still allowed to carry guns but if they use them
everyone screams, Shoot the tyres! Shoot the tyres! Don't

shoot the Brazilian in the face! This is all anyone can say
these days. But don't worry, I signed a privacy agreement
so I won't say it. I won't say anything. I'll stick to my word.

Scrooge

A baby got born in a barn! Let me buy you
an authentic model of an 18th-century sundial &
compass, an iPhone charger in the shape of a Granny
Smith apple, the world's tiniest walkie-talkie, a TV static
LED key ring, a packet of penis pasta, St Nektarious in silver
and gold at 18 x 23 cm, a call of the mountains cow figurine,
the smell of pine needles burning against the living room
window, the sweet stench of pig's blood at the butcher,
& the ability to feel something other than fiscally
responsible! Let's get loose and forget we ever
went to school! Let's dance as if we don't
have bones, and go home at midnight, alone!
Alone! The city's nut wards fill up quick this time
of year so best stick to the beds you know unless you
want to end up in Orange. It's easy to live with your back
to the world when there's blood congealed in your new iPhone.
Feeling disconnected? My friends get lost and find themselves in Asia.
India's eating Africa's rice, and everyone's carrying the Congo around
in their pockets. Look up! There are monsters in our skyscrapers
with tinsel in their hair. They are blind, but when they shut
their eyes they see the planet's capillaries pumping
straight into their left ventricles. Open your
throats wide and drink deep. The true
spirit of Christmas is 40 proof
and best drunk hidden
in a brown paper
bag.

This season

       horns are washing up on shore
and the harbour's the colour of blood. Unimaginable
concepts are yielding their evidence.

                                  Unicorns!

    Climate change!

The colour green leapt into the heart of a man
on the wrong side of the lower house. His mouth moved,
possessed, so they pushed him in case it was rabies.
Green! Green! Green! It's everywhere this summer,
burning into yellow. It's shining between escalator
teeth at your nearest department store. It's glowing
in my seaweed salad. It's somehow found its way
onto my shorts. Red algae washed in with the rain,
and now our yachts will have to get scraped.
So what if the harbour isn't green? Look! The sky
is a kind of yellowish aquamarine, when the city
isn't hacking up smog from the bottom of its CBD,
and whittle away the wood that has grown around
my ribs – there is still some sappy skerrick of
viridescence left.
        When I was a kid I couldn't understand
why farmers wouldn't superphosphate their fields
to look the way I imagined they should:

                                  green,

    green,

                green!

                  all the way up to the sky.

go home australia your drunk!!

I'm an Aussie and proud. Seems to me the Aussies are the only people that have humanity in their hearts. I work with a guy from afgahn and has been here 7 years and came through the proper channels and he thinks they should be stopped with regards to boats. And and alot of people take advantage of Aussies generosity. the fact of the matter is yes they are aloud to come here we let them live they get all that and there still not happy, its what has caused the slander and racism in my eyes. I have no problem with people from other countries immigrating to our great nation I do object to the hundreds of millions of dollars we spend on illegal immagrants when my grand mother won't turn on the air conditioning because she can't afford to the power to run as her pension is barely enough to live on as it is. we arent saying its wrong for then to have escaped their own war torn country or any of that. thats fine, just dont come here and fuck up our country.. which alot of them do because back in theres they didnt have rules to live by like we do. We could at least make the law that they have to stick by our dress codes n live by our gods or no god if they're going to come here just to preach and yet us aussies get branded racist or infidel's or fakir. Which most muslims don't even know the true meaning of what Jihad means, any muslims know what jihad means? Please tell me. Im an aussie and i educate myself on culture. Better to have a good understanding on something before i comment, that way i do not look like a fool. We are routinely taught this at uni! Since I'm a university student I receive some money from centrelink . I went there two weeks ago and this Pakistani douche bag starts yelling and screaming "you give me more money or I will go back to my own country !" They aren't all poor little refugees seeking asylum! Some if not most EXPECT to be let in and on their terms! It's now at a point where Australian children are being told "sorry we can't sing Christmas songs because little Billy over there his family don't celebrate Christmas so we can't because we might upset or offend him"!!!!! wat I have a problem with is being told "sorry u can't fly ur Aussie flags on ur car because it's going 2 offend Joe the Muslim down the street" or "sorry but we can't sing the Australian national anthem at parade anymore because little Sally over there doesn't like it"!!!!! then they change our street names to there language if they can't read it lean fucking English if we moved to Afghanistan they wouldn't fucking change there street names to suit us they wouldn't give us houses or give us the fucking doll then they wanna fucking change Australia Day to citizens day meanwhile OUR senior citizens, who fought hard to save this country in wars or who have lived her all their lives working hard in this country get nothing And another thing half of them are doctors and just give you antibiotics could be telling you your gonna die in 10 days and yet no idea what there saying. take the diseases and shit back to there country how bout making there country a better place instead of everyone running over here and start filthy gangs that carry around machetes and shit. Go for a walk down the street mate there everywhere. They are the kings at running away from problems they stink they wreck the cricket when you go there get excited of everything take people's jobs ring you up as telemarketers all the time can't understand them on the phone when you ring some place important. Plus a few of them bashed me brother when was his walking home one night for nothing there scum I'd love for it to be like America cross out borders and we can shoot u down like scummy animal u are Fuck yeah Kill the fucking dawggs JULIA GILLARD won't do nothing about it Australia the lucky country yeh to the fuks who come in illegally tax me some more ya red headed fukin mole Our government is fucked lets start our own government our prime minister is a girl for fuck sake They should throw away the key and poot the in jalee They should blow there fuckin boats up in the ocean!! Send them to nz. Australias full. Send them all to Tasmania haha kill the mutts fuck off you rotten diseased job stealing aliens, this is our land, and if you don't like what we have to say to you, get on that poorly built boat like you parents did and find somewhere else Let them die weak anyway survival of the fittest haha two many people on the earth at the moment weather you like it or not. Chinas trying to limit there kids to 1 in some places even they realise there's to many of them haha I hope some Chinese bloke rapes your mum. Straya cunts, we could be the best country in the world.

The above poem consists entirely of comments on a Facebook post from 17 December 2012 on the page "Fucken righto mate".

Cartography

In Redfern Park, in January, I could draw
circles in so many ways. This one sweeps her up
with him, as he pulls her onto the grass. That one only
curves for girls lying on their stomachs, calves swinging
like pendulums in an upside-down grandfather clock, shaken
free of regimented time. At the axis of the paths the fountain's
spray breaks light into a kaleidoscope of arcs dissolving back
into the pavers. We could do the same to circles everywhere
& watch how the people in them change when their skin
gradually twists inside out, letting other people in.
When I am long dead, I hope whoever's left
will look back at a time when countries
existed, and laugh at our quaint
need to sit in watertight
circles of our
own.

Midnight Mass

The bishop's hat is a penis,
its pallid foreskin partially

retracted from the red head
burning underneath. Priests

used to be tethered to the rack
the instant they thought of sex.

Now they have all the time of a hulking
Royal Commission to fly to Thailand

and get whipped the way they want.
Under their penises their minds must

crave something vibrant to dream about.
The censer would be a mediaeval weapon

if it weren't for the altar boy
holding the chain, swinging the ball

exactly the way he was told. The eaves
are high, the pews smooth and ready

for historical exhibit. Bring back the cat
o' nine tails! I don't trust the deacon's teeth,

and the organ player's pressing the keys
as if she's sitting for her 4th-grade AMEB.

We sing limply, each word an overcooked
vegetable sliding off our slack tongues. We

won't bust our duodenums straining for the 'Hark'
because it might hurt. It's hard to relate to a baby

born before epidurals were invented.
These days Santa divides like an amoeba

then sits on his thousand thrones in shifts.
He never needs to get nailed in order to come

back bearing
gifts.

Etymology

In time, names untether
from their namesakes. Delphiniums
once looked like dolphins. Now all we see are
flowers in colours the elderly dye their hair to match.
A stadium is a large terrarium built in order to grow men
gnarled with muscle, who chase footballs as if they were fruit
to be juiced for the elixir of life. The point is not to get the ball
over the line, the point is to create a sub-tropical climate out
of our collective breath. Tonight I will say "terrarium" until
I sleep, or at least until the word severs from its anchor
and is beautiful for no reason other than its
own sound blooming in the globe
of my mouth.
terrarium
terrarium terrarium
terrarium terrarium terrarium
terrarium terrarium terrarium terrarium
terrarium terrarium terrarium terrarium terrarium
terrarium terrarium terrarium terrarium terrarium terrarium

Now that's cricket

Sporty boy toy, hit me for six. Take off your box and carry the bat
chest on. Come to my crease, I am clean bowled. Give back your
mongoose bat. Swap it for some hoodoo in the hutch. There be
rabbits in this pie chucker and you should know there's a dead
bat in cow corner, and a diamond duck in my Dilscoop. Welcome
to the corridor of uncertainty! Here you can get your eye on a good
golden pair if you'd just be my nightwatchman. Donkey drop
into the eagle eye, find the gap between gully and slip then
follow through with five forty footwork and we're gardening
fruit salad. HOWZAT! Look, we all know cricket is another word
for standing in a field for five days, killing time between drinks.
What's the silly point? I'd rather cook your platinum duck
in my mullygrubber. Garn, flick this flipper over the fence.
Throw this maiden over your fine leg, spin your grubber up
the yipps. I don't need your tea towel explanation. I'm here
for the same reason as you. This flipper zoots along the ground
without much bounce if you don't slow ball into the Vatta Vee.
Oh! Are you a stonewaller? Like to bang it in the block hole?
We can bring in a third man, but he better know how to paddle
scoop the hot spot in my rib tickler. Or, we could swing an Indian
spin quartet? Do I have to spell it out? Hit. Your. Middle. Stump.
Into. My. Sticky. Wicket. What? Is my harrow drive too googly?
Maybe I should underarm my own bodyline; helicopter my own
sun ball to the skyline. OK fine, this has been a fun run chase,
but now you're down and out, dipper.

                                                    End of innings.

Too close for comfort

Go to the pine forest. Go walking
out amongst trees. Let their
needles tattoo your skin
by moving the hairs
on your arms,
just so. There
are three kinds
of mushrooms at your
feet; animal tracks you don't
know how to read. There are
traces of – what – traces
of fire. You are 180 km
from the ocean, but
still you know: when
the mountains are part
of the drowned world, the squid
will be at home in these deep greens,
wrapping their tentacles around our
prawn pink necks. We will be
terrified, then amazed
they ever let us
get this
close.

Broken train lines

There aren't enough poems in our newspapers,
or ballrooms on our trains.

CityRail, your evacuation procedure will be useless in the event
of an existential crisis.

This Christmas, all I am spending is time
riding the Mountains by rail.

The fluro orange safety bollards clustered by the tracks
look huddled in fear of rain.

At the summit the music swells, the trees part. A wooden boat
is stuck in the branches of a gum.

It wants a torrent to break from the clouds as remembrance of days
moved by water.

Boats in rain become basins for small oceans. And leaves
could be boats for ants.

There's a stray witch's hat by the hole in the hurricane fence. Perhaps
she took it off, carefully,

before escaping the safety zone to fly her boat
towards an ocean held as cloud.

Comb jelly

It's too hot to panic. Let the air out of your suit
and fall down the shaft of your own underwater
field of vision. The cold will hit you like a floor
smashed open by your feet. Calm
down. You can't talk here.
The fish won't listen.
Now you are subject to
a new, vague zoology. Listen
to your improbable breath, the purr
of a speedboat challenging the science
of surface tension. Forget all life lived past
where light is held like lasers in smoke. Down
here, what's three metres off passes by shadow-
like and blissfully unknowable. A fish could be the fin
of a shark. A seahorse: a rusted gun shaft tangled in net.
Jellyfish haven't changed for over five hundred million
years. Who says we need to be any more complicated?
Let's live underwater with skin two cells thick & let
thoughts crack across our bodies like a house
in permanent celebration of Christmas.
I will be egg-shaped, you will have
retractable tentacles, our young
will be loved planktonically.
Ego-less, we will be free
to drag our loose guts
behind us for all the ocean
to see. *Poor people*, we will think
in iridescent pink, *they're under such
pressure to subdue the earth.*

Marrickville cats

I know where the Marrickville cats convene at night:
on a cul-de-sac, above where the rainwater pipe
dribbles between two factories fenced off
with chicken wire. In the afternoon the cats
sit like sundials, only paying attention to time
when the light implicates them in the telling of it
and they can see their own shadows thrown down
at their feet: evidence they are the leaky gods
they know themselves to be. They often keep growing
after the sun has sunk, until they sit as tall as the ibises
in the creek – the ones drinking sewer water with old
chicken in their feathers. Once I saw a cat that didn't know
when to stop growing. It grew until its fat tail
stuck in the sewer pipe. Its meows rattled the cages
of battery hens stacked behind the corrugated iron
across the street. The giant cat thought of those rectangular,
boneless birds, and wailed at the filthy ibises to unlock
their cages so he might get fed in the manner a god
of his dimensions deserves. Riding past, I have seen
a kitten sitting on a brand new director's chair, positioned
just left of the she oak by the road. Only its eyes moved
and they moved me down the street. I have seen
the back end of a stiff cat shoved in a plastic bag
wedged between a wall and a shrub. Once I saw
no cats at all, just an old man sitting on a straight-backed
wooden chair, on the footpath above the sewer pipe,
with his nose and knees pressed against the chicken
wire fence. The next day the cats were sitting in an asymmetrical

formation, pointing their shadows towards the chair-shaped
effigy left in their temple overnight. The old man
never returned. What lingers is how his gaze ran parallel
to the line of the rainwater pipe reaching towards the sea;
how his eyes and the pipe leaked black water.

How to reason with snakes

You can't reason with snakes.
Forget what a Buddhist would say,
and cut them in half with a rake.
Worried you'll get flies? Kill them with spray.
Forget what a Buddhist would say,
or your twelve-year-old self: proud, but bow-legs
worried.
                   You get flies, kill them with spray,
and dream of snakes pulsing out ten white eggs
and your twelve-year-old self: proud, but bow-legs
black, like the corpses of flies. Because you can't plead,
you dream of snakes pulsing out ten white eggs.
You can't offer open arms, tea, or wooden beads –
black, like the corpses of flies – because you can't plead
when it comes to snakes. You *can* cover your doorways with gauze.
You *can't* offer open arms, tea, or wooden beads.
Plant traps round your gardens, ladies, because
when it comes to snakes, you can cover your doorways with gauze
or cut them in half with a rake.
Plant traps round your gardens, ladies, because
you can't reason with snakes.

An ode to the stupidity of sheep

You can see why no one would let a sheep
into their house. Their eyes are like giant

oysters gorged on grit and sit
too far apart. They glare as you

walk the full ten metres towards them, then scamper
as though you materialised from a cloud of gunpowder

and extra-terrestrial light. Their hooves pound the earth,
trying to tame it. Oh please. We don't need another England:

small and clammy and cleansed of any animals that pose
a challenge to our farming practices. I want to keep

wild things that can't be fenced. Roos outnumber us 3:1.
It's a wonder they let us carry on as if we owned the place.

If they could be bothered they'd put their paws
on our foreheads and watch us punch the air

between our barrel chests, but instead
they occasionally let themselves get killed

so we can keep thinking we're the ones
behind the wheel. When will they stop

shirking their responsibilities as lords
and masters? I wish I could remember

what the world was like before I had a language
for its bits and pieces. Perhaps a sheep and a roo

just looked animal. A bluebottle
is two different organisms: one

at the head and one bringing up
the rear, and yet all we see is one

more reason not to go swimming. Truth be told
we'd all keel over if it weren't for the billions

of bugs in our guts, so we're
hardly flying solo ourselves.

The little things

Ever since the dinosaurs died, we predators have been downsizing.
Now we are lost in a soup of quarks.

Of course nothing makes sense when you hold your nose
up to the glass. The world is a magic eye

and you have to retreat slowly with a soft focus if you want to see
everything jitterbug together.

There is a cuckoo from the PNG with a squawk that could knock the flesh
off a dead man's bones. It strips the bark

off trees, unsettles insects in their exoskeletons. It lays eggs in other
birds' nests and its chicks kill off

the host bird's brood by monopolising the distribution of food. This bird
may be small in comparison to dinosaurs,

but its call is larger than the whole valley. The sound is a brutal
ripping open of the throat and leaves

a gash in time. I can see my parents' house from here, as nothing more
than a T-Rex's footprint,

and those gums as shrubs next to the ghosts of Wollemis towering above.
When we're all dead

the micro-organisms will take us down, while the ants bike it out of here,
or bandy together to build nests

in our hollowed out
suits.

Plum tree

My mother's brain is spotted white. They say
it's nothing, but sometimes she says "gang bang"
when we're talking about gardening, then giggles.

There's a town six hours north called Graves End
where the streets have no trees. There,
pensioners refuse to die. The government has to buy

antennas for their TVs, or else they'll climb out
their windows at dusk and roam the streets,
looking for water. What shall we do? I shall

rush out as I am, and walk the streets with my hair
down, so. Ah, I said the wrong thing again,
but this time it was Eliot. Poetry's just not *practical*,

'though I reckon we'll have all the time of our own
decomposition to be of practical use to the worms,
so why waste it now, filing statutory declarations?

I have corpses in my garden that are sprouting new leaves.
I wonder what the saplings will grow to be? Once, a plum tree
grew behind my grandmother's house. Each autumn it bore such

luscious fruit, she'd make plum jam for months. At winter's end
its bare twigs pushed out buds along the bark. In spring
the blossoms were lanterns, trapping light from the moon.

The tree lit up the yard so my grandmother couldn't sleep.
She had only one daughter, my mother, and stopped
writing poetry after *the Bulletin* said it was doggerel.

This daughter grew. She stitched her own yellow
silk blossoms round the hem of her wedding dress,
then left, and didn't come back for months.

When she did, Gonny was kneeling over the plum
tree stump, sobbing. *It was too beautiful,*
she said. *How could I stand it any more?*

When I was born her hair turned violet.
It curled back from her face like petals
fainting against the stem. Don't ask me

what I've read, I forget everything.
Don't ask me what I know, I only know
I don't know much. But I can tell you

my wise mother has spots on her brain the colour
of plum blossoms, and sometimes gets her words wrong.
Perhaps wisdom is not an accumulation of facts,

but an opening up of the earth.

Biology

In Oberon, trees reach out from the parched earth
like tuning forks ready to sound
at the touch of lightning. Out here there are more
shades of brown and yellow than
words in the English dictionary. The tank is empty.
The creek is low. It's hard to love
what's dead. I am out of tune with this adopted country.
My great-great-grandparents, illiterate
in ochre tones, drove wooden stakes into a vampire earth
only the locals knew how to read
for lifelines.

Last autumn, while shaking the shrivelled
brains of walnuts free from their
wooden skulls, my quiet grandfather spoke. He told me
about an ancestor of ours
from South Australia. Well-respected judge and governor,
home-brewer and amateur
phrenologist, he believed he could read a man's head
the way the wind reads crests
and gullies. He offered a free case of booze for any stray
heads found rolling around
where the country hadn't yet been fenced. One day an elder
came to the door holding
the head of his wife by the hair. Her neck was still dripping,
her eyes wet and luminous as pearl.
My grandfather laughed: *The things Abos will do for a case of booze!*

There is something of this man
in my blood. My mother used to line our laundry shelves with jars
of spiders floating in methylated spirits.
She collected any funnel-web she could catch in the kitchen after rain.
Our laundry was a 19th-century
laboratory of wild things conquered by the mind. Even now
our shelves are lined with walnut fruit
turning purple in tall clear jars. They look like the pickled testes
of captured men.

To my illiterate eyes,
the history book of the hills beyond the orchard just looks
singed. I would like to think
I am not so arrogant to believe in the singular authority
of what I have been taught.
I can almost see how a spirit might live in a tree, how the earth
operates on a plane of intelligence
incompatible with the database of empirical fact we call knowledge.
I wish I could read these hills,
teach old men to feel, I wish we could see beyond the limits
of our own biology.

Ghosts make good material

B is the name of a range in Alaska. B is also the name
of my friend from Katoomba. There is a new man in the house
her father built. Old church eaves & second hand windows –
every imperfection tells its own story. He is still written
on the inside of an unfinished cupboard. He is filed away
in boxes; the boxes fill the hall. There is a new man there
who has turned her dad into a history project. His research includes:
eating in Mr B's kitchen, sleeping with Mr B's wife, getting punched
by Mr B's son. Now he finds it harder to see straight. In Katoomba,
spring can get its wires crossed. Steal a day from winter, slam it up
against a summer storm. B's mother is sick. Her mother is shedding
hair like pine needles, and in October her brother got lost in the snow,
guided by the light of his own private ghosts. When I called B
she was standing in the middle of the highway, watching wheels
lose their traction; cars swerve off into forest. They say the Devil
loves a wilderness, but my friend B is the only woman I know
who can sit where the wavelengths are low, and never let the Devil in.
Sometimes she goes off into tundra. Home of the reindeer herders.
Home of the musk ox and arctic hare. No trees can grow there,
the summers are too short. A wildfire once burned across the tundra
of the Alaskan B, but my B has learned to leave things at a smoulder.
Her brother's tundra is melting, releasing gasses. Her brother's visions
light up the rooms of their father's house with the power of all his
synapses at once. They say methane in our lamps was to blame
for all our murky, Victorian ghosts – so when the permafrost melts,
let's all get gassed and raise the dead together. Some days B rides
the train downhill so she can drink at sea level. Then she speaks

of the dead. She tells me she went for a walk behind the house,
and passed through a field of zombies. *What are you doing?*
they moaned. *Walking home,* she said, *what are you doing?*
They put down their arms, stopped frothing at the mouth.

Oh, we're just making a movie, hey.

The red disk

A large red disk stood in the middle of the room.
We tried to walk past as if we had larger disks

in our own homes, but the disk caught our shapes
and held them upside-down; jolted us off the floor

so that we stood on different planes of existence.
How can you be so calm when your feet don't

touch the ground? I am worried the many jack-in-the-boxes
constantly exploding under my skin will give my nervous

spectre away. I am never good at being still. I need every word
I write to be liked and ten men to dance with me at all times,

or I'll vanish. You glide when others run, and make breakfast
holding a steady disk of light between the bones of your pelvis,

as though breakfast was a martial art
you mastered by accident. On this first

adventure outdoors, Anish Kapoor showed us
the void in a rock and bent us into the crooks

of his giant steel S. We learnt
how much of ourselves

there is in an image,
and how easily

images disappear
in just one step.

Soon we were checking over our shoulders, wanting to touch
the forbidden, to cross the marked line on the floor. We were

melting in mirrors, being eaten by a red glaze, losing ourselves
in our own reflections. It must be hard to make art that strips

adults of their cocked eyebrows and deflationary sentences.
Afterwards, the only thing our addled brains could process

was the sensory information of grass
pressing into our backs. Now I'm not

sure where I stand
in relation to voids.

The earth spins
                                        faster the closer
                    you get
        to the still
                                        centre. The sculpture

            shifted us

around and I don't
                                        even know
                    your middle

        name.

Bikies

Bikies are rough as guts
but I know guts
aren't rough
they're smooth
as sausages, pink
as a string of unborn
rats, tender as a triple
bypassed heart.

Watertight

When we arrived, we got piles from shagging on the shag pile.
We visited the hen-pecked dinners in their pens; the penguins

rising like war from the waves. Then we killed the lemon verbena.
I thought it was Vietnamese mint. All herbs look the same

when they're dried into sticks. Now I'm certain the multiverse
spirals out from your solar plexus. We were living in a world

you'd dreamt up months before. That's why
I was ten fathoms behind my own face.

Melbourne in winter is a clenched fist, its fingernails painted
black. I will leave you a purple heart, but not for bravery.

There were no bats to make us look up
out of our borrowed yard, and everything was frightening,
                                                especially blank paper.
You froze you actually froze.

But I still remember the way my hands
fit in your chest

                two leaves
                in a cup

which once held water.

Keeping it real *with Kendrick Lamar*

wake up

    I do what I wanna do, I say what I wanna say

    when I feel, and I

check twitter

    look in the mirror and know I'm there

get up

    with my hands in the air, I'm proud to

check twitter

    say yeah

    I'm real, I'm real, I'm

                                     barely awake

make coffee in undies

    in a world that

check facebook

    come with plan B

drink coffee leaning against kitchen bench staring at wall

    cause plan A never

check emails

    your plans only can

open fridge, stare at contents, close fridge

    pan around love

    you love him, you love them, you –

check twitter

    when love hurts

and bread for mould

    even if they fell

    out the sky and your optics turn stale

put two slices in toaster

    where they mold that's green

check twitter
I promise that I know you
open cupboard, take peanut butter off shelf
I can see you
register smell of rotting onion, close cupboard
when it all breaks you, you still
check twitter
love them and
spread peanut butter on toast
you love
while tweeting
keepin' control
of everything
wipe peanut butter off
you love
twitter
might even love it to death

On the 36th floor

we are on par with thunder.
The clouds are switched to reverse,
hoovering steam from the craniums
of CEOs. They're holding shit together
just beneath the spires of skyscrapers,
channelling gold fever, sucking lifts
up shafts with every morning coffee-
run. And then where does it go?
Get scrambled by the flurry of bats
above the bridge? Shoot rocks
down from the solar system? Listen,
I'm not trying to tell you anything
you don't already know. I saw you
watch that woman try to push back
the bones round her eyes, and we've
all been caught in the tiny electrical
storms of kitchenette etiquette wars.
There must be more than two million
people stashed behind those windows:
wired up, plugged in and terrified
of their own numerical inventions.
Zoom out and you'll see the same red pop up
everywhere, lacing flags to lights to trees
that just won't let go of their leaves,
strapping the city in place, so nothing
kicks round the universe when the earth
tips at the end of the day. What we might lose:
decimals culled from rounding down,
ideas cut loose from interrupted

conversations, your Disnified
musical future, blasted to bits
and shuddering, dehydrated,
in the air conditioning vent,
about
       to lose
            its grip.

For Tim

Back covered in grass, you were rocketing
down the road in shorts, boots, a bowler hat
and your then future mother-in-law's cardigan.
It flew out behind you like a superhero's cape
that can't help reaching back
towards the people it leaves behind.
Your eyebrows were pin-balling up
and down under the rim of your hat, oh yes
you were alive that night, imagination turbo
charged, DTs making your hands dart forward
for once. Next, we were flat on our backs
on the Rushcutters grass, like frogs catapulted
onto a high gravity planet. Perhaps it was
the onshore breeze that woke us up. Perhaps
that near-by tree really was a full lung, breathing
the world into us, holding it there, until we had
climbed our way through all it could catch in its branches.
Or it was your cerebral cortex, flooded with blood,
connecting this to that to things that haunted you
in your blue childhood room. Lying on our backs
we were cockroach gods, fingers and the sheer
damn force of our nuclear-proof minds moving
the stars around, throwing new constellations
into focus. We were mapping new territories,
arguing about legal dramas. You were certain
some of them were good. I was adamant
they're misrepresentative of this tangled mess
we find ourselves living in. And anyway,
just how many lawyers do you know? Why do *they*

get to represent *us*? We sat up and not even fifteen
minutes had passed. We'd realigned the solar system,
re-written Boston Legal, all in a quarter of an hour.

Now, I'm driving to Bathurst for reception.
The last time we spoke, you told me you were
on the wrong pills, couldn't sit still and watched
the walls move, 'cause it was safer than sleeping.

Here, it's late spring, and the grass is sprinting
towards summer. Last night, gunshots bounced
back and forth between the hills. I dreamt
of walruses launching out from a sea wall
and swimming through water thick with black crabs
as large as men's torsos. In the morning, the two flies
I'd left humming on the sill were twenty screaming circles
high up near the ceiling, seeing thousands of themselves,
and busting their wings, repeatedly, against the walls.

There are rabbits I think about trapping for you,
so they don't turn up: a dried out ear jaw foot
and twisted stomach. And the sky here is so broad
it's like the fat end of a telescope. Everything in Sydney
is miniature and movable and makes me shout
of course! but shout from somewhere cellular,
that doesn't know a language I can write,
or you can read.

Punch lines

We never knew when to laugh. One afternoon
We were sitting on the cushions he used as a makeshift bed.
We were turning his problems into punch lines.
      He was too, and laughing like a machine gun firing at the roof.
We relaxed, as much as you can under fire.
We thought, *Ah! The problem is us!*
We take him too seriously, when he is only joking!
We need to be less dramatic!!!
We chose not to notice how his nails were orange at the quicks.
We leant back in our chairs, felt the muscles in our necks relax, as they do
      when the lights go up at the movies and although you've been bawling,
      you realise no one you know has actually died.
We were quiet, savouring the lightness of our new discovery. One of us may
      have gone to make a salad. I shut my eyes for a second, and opened them
      to find his blue eyes pried open, fist poised at the side of his head,
      not yet covered in blood.

Arrogant ghost,

you chose to haunt us in absentia
so you could get maximum coverage. Now everything

is full of your absence. You are not hovering, Matrix-style,
above your house when I drive past. You are not swinging

from the switched-on light bulb in your room. I can't
feel you in the velvet drag of the armchair beside

your bed. You are not beaming out from your still-active
profile picture. You are not lurking in my cupboards.

You are not in the safe-house of my memory,
because my memory has never been safe.

You cannot be conjured from the shared
genes expressed in your sister's face.

You are not anywhere, which is exactly
where you wanted to be.

Death metal

I'm writing to tell you
your mother ordered a strong cappuccino and a biscuit
so she's doing okay.

She told me things you'd hate me to know. Like how,
when you saw Santa at Westfield, you pumped your three-year-old fists
as if you were at the Ramones. It's hard

to trust trains after Auschwitz.
Cities haven't always looked out for their denizens. Even now
we send men with guns and cuffs

to take the terrified and alone to hospital.
Your mother wants to understand what kept you
up at the mauve hours. I told her

your flatmate heard you howling
like a husky in a sweltering zoo. And now, how easily life meanders on.
Four million people writhing together

does not one megasoul make. I'm gonna go
to the SCG where we lose our minds like Romans braying for Christian blood.
When we're drunk it'll almost be like

we're alive and killing our own meat again.
Outside our stadiums: the effortless alchemy of mundane interactions.
Men you could have been are choking

in their own neckties, painstakingly
separating numbers from the precious metals
they used to represent. I will never

forget the night my face
peeled open like aluminium foil, and you saw nothing
under my cheekbones.

Sleeper train

Dipping in and out of the slow wave stage
memories linger, fly out the window
and splatter against the side of the train.

If you don't sleep deep you won't remember
anything you learned during the day. After a week
of being buffeted around by half-remembered plans,

I find myself on a sleeper train to Melbourne,
lying on a bunk above a woman I don't know, slow
cooking in the steam of her simmering thoughts.

> *I didn't know the room would be this small.*
> *Did you know the room would be this small?*
> *I didn't know the room would be this small.*

Last time I trained it south I forgot how to breathe
and called my friend for help. He yelled, JUST DON'T
PANIC! IT'S IMPORTANT TO STOP PANICKING!

> *What's this? What are these? Towels?*
> *Are they a gift? Can we keep them?*
> *This is like being on an ocean liner.*

I wish I could call him now, so he could hear how
relatively simple breath is when you're still alive.
History repeats because we never remember

the advice we give our friends when we're half
asleep. History repeats because no one's really
slept since we started sleeping alone, with all

the street lights on. We have built our own
rooms and then halls between those and then
rooms for our separate activities as well.

> *You didn't know we'd get towels? I just*
> *didn't think the room would be this small.*
> *Can we sleep with the door open?*

I dimly remember the tunnel running under my old flat –
a relic from a time when Sydney ran deep. Some people
have heard of these tunnels, but few can remember why

they lace up our separated rooms from beneath.
So many people sleep never knowing they could
leave their bodies, sink beneath the streets

and mingle with other drowned souls
fallen from skeletons to depths
never recollected in the morning.

> *I'll put this here and that there and you can change it if you like.*
> *What's this? What is this, do you think? It looks like plastic.*
> *A lot of plastic containers sitting inside each other.*

I dreamed – or I think I dreamed – we had stopped –
or we did stop – half way to Melbourne, maybe Albury,
for a midnight snack. The only place lit was a bakery

with a red and white awning, buried under the branches
of an old pepper tree. The bakery was one long aisle
running deep into the tree trunk, with sweet tarts

and glazed buns piled on either side. The woman
from the bunk beneath was standing close, but we
couldn't speak because the cakes were overflowing

with sugared flowers and chocolate-coated
rind in a way that made a person feel at sea
without a glimpse of land for reference. I could

taste enzymes. My bed was tilting.
The contents of my stomach swayed
in the opposite direction. Underneath

the woman was awake and talking
to herself. I have been lost in this place before,
I thought, but couldn't remember when.

      Oh it's a cup. See that? They fold up and make a cup.
      Oh that's ingenious. See that? Yes, that's very clever.
      A cup. That folds up. Please don't shut the door.

It's hard to remember where you're going once you learn
the points you leave are never fixed, but it's a comfort to know
nothing moves forward, either. The sun that set on Sydney

will rise in Melbourne and flood the flat streets
with a brighter, drier heat. The paint flakes
differently there, but it still flakes. Maybe

we'll remember where we're going
once we've remembered what we've
left. Both memories are loud enough

to drown the other out.

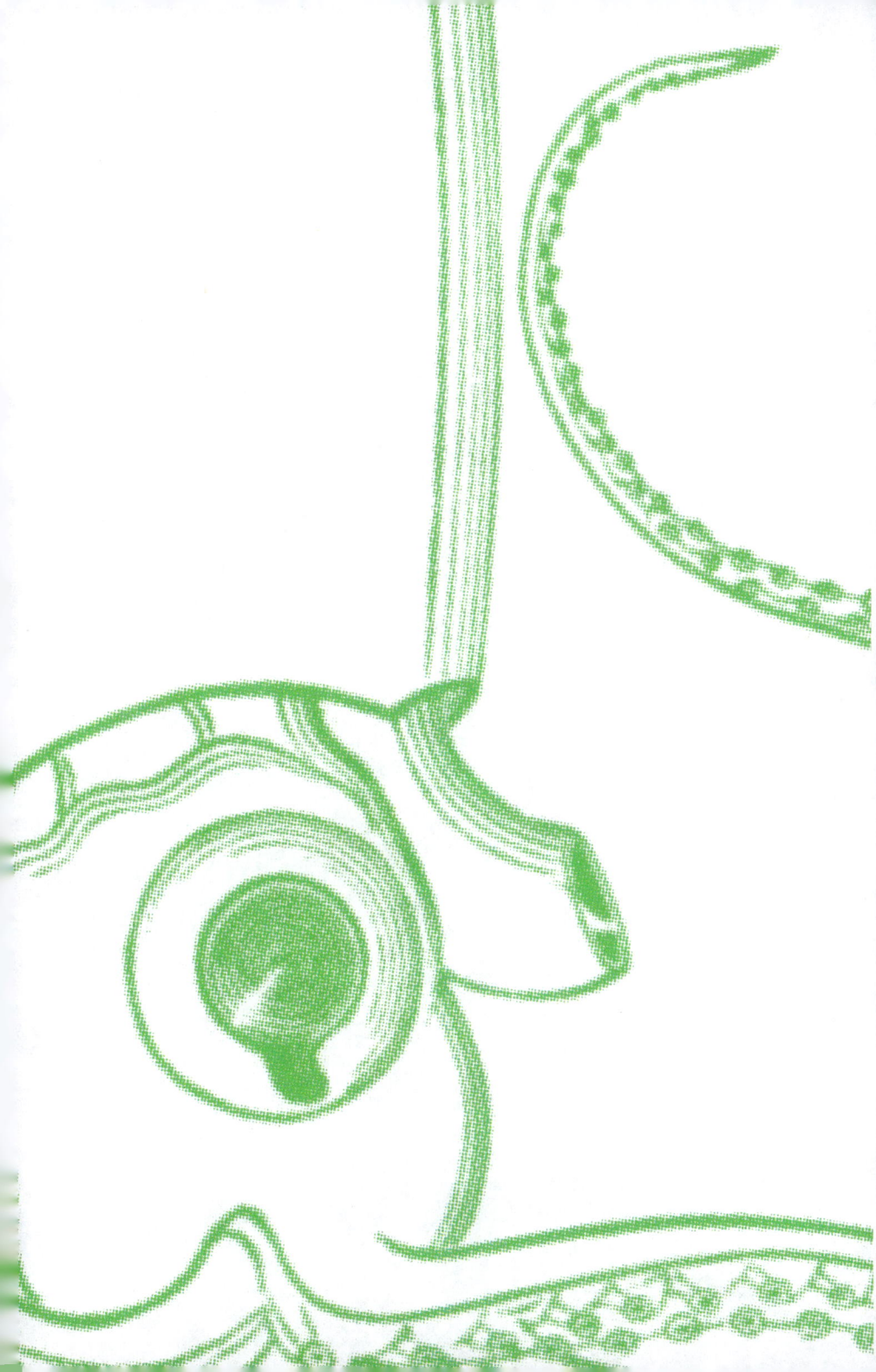

HOWL, for Allen Ginsberg

I see the best minds of my generation destroyed by
    boredom: fat, comatose, ugg-booted,
or jogging through Sydney Park at dawn
    lowering their body mass index.
Angular-haired hipsters chewing the fat till two,
    lubing the cogs of the machinery of night.
    And my school friends
who passed through universities with distinction averages
    just so they'd get into law
who were *never* expelled from the academies for crazy
    & only ever wrote meta-critique graffiti
    on the back of toilet doors,
who cower in their bosses offices with boutique
    underwear under their suits, burning
    their money on rent and listening to the terror
    of their mothers on the phone,
who eat $30 salads in gastroporn pubs and drink Semillon
    at the Ivy, or purge their body-image night after night
with MX, with botox, with hair irons, spray tan
    and coke and speedballs,
shuddering with anxiety and lightning in the mind
    leaping toward poles of Mania and Depression,
    illuminating all the motionless world
    of Home & Away emotions in-between,
Temazepan solidities of boyfriends, terrace house grey
    courtyard breakfasts, Vomit-bearded homeless
    stilettoed over in the gutter, 7/11 pit stops
    for tomorrow's comedown joyride, southern
    cross utes wolf whistling through traffic lights,

pupils as big as suns and moons and tree shivers
in the roaring winter dawns of Kings Cross, where
Cronulla blondes shriek and jocks drink out of mind,
who pay for taxis with plastic for the endless ride to Castle Hill
on pingers until the noise of sisters and children
brings them down shuddering mouth-shrivelled
and bruised, bleak of brain all drained of brilliance
in the tea-and-biscuits light of home,
who prefer to circle whole nights round the light of Kinsella's,
swim out and sit through the muddled vodka blues
of an afternoon at Icebergs,
who talk continuously about haircuts seventy hours
from work to pad to bar to Bellevue Hill to Mosman
then back across the Harbour Bridge,
whose boyfriends are lost warriors jumping down the steps
of strip clubs off balconies off bridges out of Saturn's return,
smashing their phones, screaming, vomiting, whispering slippery facts
blissfully free of the shocks of hospitals and jails and wars,
whole intellects choked up with numbers numbers numbers
and total recall for seven days and nights of sales targets
met and meat trays won on Christmas
party pink harbour cruises,
who vanish into the nowhere of themselves
leaving a trail of ambiguous picture messages
from the lost island of Atlantis,
who remember South-East Asian sweatshops
and global warming as three units of HSC
requirements filled, while international
students from China are still buried one
on top of the other in a Chippendale shoebox room,
who wander around and around the Escher stairwells of Oxford St
wondering where to go, then go, leaving no broken hearts,

who crave cigarettes on trains
    snaking through mist towards
    their parents' lonesome hobby farms.

    And the idealists
who disappear into the volcanoes of theory
    leaving behind nothing but the shadow
    of their hearts and the lava and ash of obscure
    poetry burned in the basements of Fisher Library,
who *re*appear on the internet writing incomprehensible blogs
    about how their lives inevitably lead to the writing
    of incomprehensible blogs – in beards and shorts
    with big activist eyes basted in MacBook Pro light,
who when they were teenagers burned smilies in their arms
    protesting the neurotic Capitalist prison
    of their grandparents' paradigms,
who distributed Refugee Action pamphlets at UTS weeping
    and undressing while *no* sirens wailed them down,
who broke down crying at Crown Casino naked and trembling
    before apathetic cops,
who bit detectives in the neck and shrieked with delight
    in police cars for committing no crime
    but their own wild striving to wake up,
who howled on their knees at Villawood
    and were dragged off the roof
    waving panties and manifestoes,
who desperately wanted to be fucked in the arse
    by a Malaysian people-smuggler,
    in budgie-smugglers,
    and scream with joy,
who folk-sung through the mornings, the evenings,
    in rose gardens and the grass
    of Camperdown Memorial Park

singing fragments of their shattered hearts

in the faces of whoever walked past,

And the art scensters,

who lost their boyloves to the three old shrews of CoFA

the one-eyed shrew of *Vice* magazine

the one-eyed shrew that glints in OzCo's womb

and the one-eyed shrew that does nothing but

sit on her arse and snip the intellectual golden

threads of every other craftsman's loom,

who conceptualise static and ironise with a longneck of

VB, a groupie, a pouch of baccy, some papers,

and fall off their stool and roll out of the Townie door

and down the street and end fainting

at the feet of their own vision of ultimate wit and cum

proclaiming the last gyzym of hyper-meta-consciousness,

who have sweetened the snatches of a million girls trembling

beneath gallery fluros, and were dead-eyed in the morning

but prepared to sweeten the snatch of the sunrise,

flashing buttocks under blankets and cooking

facon naked in the kitchen,

who go out whoring through the MCA in myriad

stolen coats,

who feel faded out by blockbusters, are shifted in

dreams, wake to a sudden dull Marrickville, and

pick themselves up out of basements hung-

over with heartless *talk* and horrors of CBD

stainless-steal dreams & stumble to Centrelink,

who walk all night with their shoes full of blood

waiting for a door in the street malls to open

to a room full of heady sweat and pot,

And the acting grads who create great suicidal dramas
    set in the government housing blocks of East
    London, or Baltimore under the wartime blue
    floodlight of the moon & their heads
    shall be crowned with spray-painted cardboard
    before empty theatre-houses ever more,
who eat the vindaloo of other people's imaginations
    or digest prawns from the muddy floor
    of Kevin Jackson's house,
who weep at the romance of the streets with their pushcarts
    full of onions and bad accents,
who eat rotten kangaroo lung heart feet tail meat pies & kebabs
    in ads, dreaming of pure vegetarian futures,
who Shakespeared in Albury, who died in Albury, who came back to Albury
    & waited in vain, who watched over Albury and brooded & looned
    in Albury and finally went away to find out what the rest of the world
    was doing & now Albury is lonesome for actors,
who plunge themselves under meat trucks looking for an objective,
who fly to Edinburgh forty-eight hours to find out if they have a vision or you
    have a vision or he had a vision to find out why the hell we're here,
who cut their wrists three times successively unsuccessfully,
    give up and are forced to open talent agencies
    where they think they are growing old and cry,
who sing out of their car windows in despair, cry into their agents'
    cashmeres, dance at Pure Platinum for attention, smash
    compilations of nostalgic Lloyd Webber medleys,
    finish their dates' whiskeys and throw up groaning
    into the bloody toilet, to an absence of colossal applause,

Ah, Allen, while we are not safe, you are not safe, and now you're
    really in the total animal soup of time –
I have taken the absolute heart of your poem of life and butchered it
    out of your own body

    good to eat a thousand years.

Acknowledgements

"How to reason with snakes" first appeared in the Chapbook *How to Reason with Snakes and other poems*, published by Picaro Press in 2011.

"HOWL, for Allen Ginsberg" borrows its structure from "HOWL, for Carl Solomon" by Allen Ginsberg, and was written for the Story Club event "The Sincerest form of Flattery" in 2011, and was performed at the National Young Writers' Festival in the same year, and the Sydney Writers' Festival in 2013.

"On the 36th floor" was published in the Sydney issue of *Cordite* in May, 2012.

The poems "Now that's cricket", "Plum tree", "Biology", "Ghosts make good material", "This season", "Happy Christmas! (don't get tasered)", "Watertight", "Scrooge", "All that's left to discuss", "Broken train lines", "Midnight Mass", "Comb jelly", "An ode to the stupidity of sheep", "Bikies", "The red disk", "The little things", "Etymology", "go home australia your drunk!!", "Cartography", "Too close for comfort", "Marrickville cats", "Keeping it real *with Kendrick Lamar*", "Punch lines", "Death metal", "Sleeper train", and "Arrogant ghost" first appeared on the Lifted Brow's website over the summer of 2012–13. Many thanks are due to Sam Cooney for his encouragement and editorial rigour.